THE DOCTRINE OF ADDAI THE APOSTLE

The Armenian Version

Edited and translated from Old Armenian by
Daniel Deleanu

LogoStar Press

Toronto

Hare Krishna!

ISBN: 978-1-105-77024-1

Printed and bound in the USA.

On the epistle of King Abgar,[1] *the son of King Ma'nu, and the time he sent it to our Master who was in Jerusalem; and the time Addai the Apostle*[2] *came to him [Abgar]who dwelt in Urha;*[3] *and what he spoke in his gospel; and what he said and commanded, when he departed from this world, to those who had inherited from him the blessings of the priesthood.*

In the year three hundred and forty-three of the Seleucid Era,[4] and in the dominion of our master Tiberius, the Roman Emperor, and in the dominion of King Abgar, son of King Ma'nu, in the month of October, on the twelfth day, Abgar Ukkama sent Marihab and Shomshagrom,[5] high officials and dignitaries from his kingdom, and Hanan, the archive keeper, to the city known [in Greek] as Eleutheropolis, but in Aramaic as Beth Gubrin,[6] to the great

---

[1] King Abgar is called here "the son of Ma'nu"; however, it is difficult to know exactly which Ma'nu this was, since there was more than one ruler by this name.

[2] The Roman historian Eusebius of Caesarea (c. CE 263 – 339), also called Eusebius Pamphili, states in his *Ecclesiastical History* (i.13 and iii.1) that Addai was one of the seventy disciples of Christ.

[3] The Syriac name of Urha (Եդեսիա) was Edessa (ܐܘܪܗ).

[4] The Seleucid era, or *Anno Graecorum* (literally "Year of the Greeks"), was a system of numbering years in use by the Seleucid Empire and other countries among the ancient Hellenistic civilizations. The era dates from the return of Seleucus I Nicator to Babylon in 311 BC after his exile in Ptolemaic Egypt, considered by Seleucus and his court to mark the founding of the Seleucid Empire. The introduction of the new era is mentioned in one of the Babylonian Chronicles, *The Chronicle of the Diadochi*.

[5] This name in the Syriac version is Shamshagram.

[6] Sometimes spelled Beth-gubrin, or Beth'gubrin.

Sabinus, the son of Eustorgius, the second-in-command to our master the emperor, who ruled over Syria, Phoenicia, Israel, and the whole country of Mesopotamia. They brought him epistles regarding the affairs of the empire; and when they reached him, he received them with enjoyment and much nobility, and they stayed with him for twenty-five days. He composed for them a reply to the epistles, and sent them to King Abgar. When they departed from him, they headed towards Jerusalem; and they saw many people, who came from far away to see Christ, because the eminence of his great deeds had travelled to the remotest of lands. When Marihab, Shomshagrom, and Hanan, the keeper of the archives, saw those people, they joined those strangers on the way to Jerusalem.

Upon entering Jerusalem, they saw Christ, and they rejoiced with the whole hosts, who were always around Him. But they also saw the Jewish priests, who were standing in groups, and pondering what they should do to Him; for they were disturbed to see that a great many of their people confessed Him. And they stayed in Jerusalem for ten days, and Hanan, the keeper of the archives, recorded everything he witnessed Christ doing: nothing that He did escaped him until they set off. And then they departed, and went to Urha, wherein they presented themselves before King Abgar, their own ruler who had sent them, and they gave him the reply to the epistles, which they had brought with them. After the epistles were read, they began to give the king an account of all they had witnessed and all deeds Christ had performed in Jerusalem. And Hanan, the keeper of the archives, read before him all he had recorded and brought along. And when King Abgar heard the accounts, he was amazed and marvelled, and so were his princes, who stood before him. Abgar then said to them, "These impressive works are not human, but they come from God; for no one from this world can make the dead alive again, except for God. And Abgar expressed his wish to pass over and head to Israel, and witness with his own eyes all those miracles Christ was working; but since he was not able to pass through the land of the Romans, which he did not rule over, lest this cause hostility, he wrote an epistle and sent it to Christ by the hand of Hanan, the keeper of the archives.

He left behind Urha on the fourteenth day of March, and entered Jerusalem on the twelfth day of April, on the fourth day of the week.[7] And he found Christ at the house of Gamaliel, the chief-priest[8] of the Jews. The epistle was opened before Him, and read thus: "Abgar Ukkama, to Jesus, the Good Healer, who has appeared in the land of Jerusalem. Peace, my Master! I have heard of You and of Your healing, that it is not by medicines and roots that You heal, but by Your word You open the eyes of the blind, You make the crippled able to walk, cleanse the lepers, and make the deaf capable of hearing. And You heal by Your word the mad who are possessed by unclean spirits,[9] and those who are troubled; You also bring the dead to life. And when I heard of these great miracles that You work, I said to myself that either You are God, who has come down from heaven and performs all these deeds, or You are the

[7] On a Wednesday.

[8] The Armenian word is "chief"; nevertheless, the word refers to the highest authority of the Jews.

[9] Demonic spirits.

Son of God, who does all these wonders. Thus, I have written to request of You to come to me, the one who worships You, and to heal the disease which I have, as I have belief in You. This also I have heard, that the Jewish priests mutter against You and harass You, and would even like to crucify You, and seek to treat You heartlessly. I am ruler over one small but beautiful city, and it is more than enough for both to dwell therein peacefully."

When Jesus took possession of the epistle at the residence of the chief-priest of the Jews, He said to Hanan, the keeper of the archives: "Go and say to your master, who has sent you to Me, 'Blessed are you, who, even though you have not seen Me, believe in Me, for it is written[10] of Me, <Those who see Me shall not believe in Me, and those who see Me not, shall believe in me>.[11] But as to that which you have written to Me, namely that I should come to you, that for which I was sent here is now completed, and I am going up to my Father, who sent me, and when I am with Him, I will send to you one of my disciples, and he will cure the disease which you have, and restore your good health; and all who are with you he will convert to eternal life. Your city shall be blessed, and no enemy shall ever triumph over it again.'"

When Hanan, the keeper of the archives, saw that Jesus spoke to him like that, since he also was the king's

---

[10] From the expression "it is written," one could infer that this passage is from the *Old Testament*, but in reality it is not. The author obviously refers to another text, which remains mysterious. However, this unknown text must have been considered to be canonical since the author gives it as reference.

[11] "Those who see Me shall not believe in Me, and those who see Me not, shall believe in me" is from John 20:29.

painter, he began to paint a portrait of Jesus with a variety of paints, and brought it with him to King Abgar, his master. And when King Abgar saw the portrait, he received it with much happiness, and placed it with great honour in one of his palace's compounds. Hanan, the keeper of the archives, related to him all he had heard from Jesus, as His words had been put by him in writing. After Christ had ascended to heaven, Judas Thomas[12] sent to Abgar Addai the Apostle, who was one of the seventy-two apostles. And when Addai came to the city of Urha, he lodged in the house of Tobias,[13] the son of Tobias the Jew, who was from Israel. Word of his arrival spread throughout the land, and one of the nobles of Abgar, by the name of Abdu,[14] the son of Abdu, one of those who had kneeled before Abgar, went and spoke the following words about Addai: "Behold, a messenger has come, and lodges here, he of whom Jesus said to you, "I send to You one of my disciples." And when Abgar heard these words, and of the impressive deeds which Addai had performed, and of the amazing healings which he had carried out, he reckoned, "Verily, this is he whom Jesus sent, saying, 'When I have ascended to heaven I will send to you one of my disciples, and he will heal your disease.'"

---

[12] The mention of Judas in the text confirms that it was the Apostle Thomas, and not another Thomas, that who sent Addai to Urha.

[13] The Armenian historian Moses of Khoren (ca. 410-490 AD), author of the famous *History of Armenia*, claims that Tobias had not renounced Judaism, but simply followed its laws until he converted to Christianity.

[14] The same Moses of Khoren (see the previous note) describes Abdu as "greatly honoured in all the palace of the king."

Abgar, therefore, sent for Tobias, and said to him, "I have heard that a stranger who possesses great powers has come, and has taken lodging in your house. Bring him to me, for he is my great hope of recovery." Tobias went early on the next morning and took Addai the Apostle, whom he brought to Abgar. Addai himself was aware that he had been sent there by the power of God. And when Addai came up and went to Abgar, who was in the company of his nobles, and in heading towards him, Abgar had a magnificent vision before Addai. Once Abgar's vision had started, he kneeled down before Addai and worshipped him. Great astonishment seized all those who were standing before him, for they could see nothing of the vision which was being seen by Abgar. Then Abgar said to Addai, "You truly are the disciple of Jesus, that powerful one, the son of God, who sent one to me saying, 'I send you one of my disciples for curing your disease and for obtaining life eternal.'"

Addai said to him, "Since you believed from the very beginning in Him who sent me to you, for that reason I have been sent to you, and if you believe in Him, everything in which you do believe, you shall have."

Abgar said to him, "So I have believed in Him; and with respect to those Jews who crucified Him, I am ready to take an army with me, and go and chastise them; but because the kingdom belongs to the Romans, I am restrained by the covenant of peace, which has been validated by me with our master, the emperor Tiberius, just like my forefathers."

Addai said to him, "Our Master has fulfilled the will of His Father. And when He had carried out the will of His

Father, He was taken up to Him, and sat with Him in glory, with whom he was from since the beginning of time."

Abgar said to him, "I also believe in Him and in His Father."

Addai said to him, "Because you possess so much faith, I place my hand on you, in the name of Him in whom you believe." At the moment he placed his hand upon him, he was cured of the terrible affliction which he had been plagued by for a long time.[15]

Abgar was astonished and wondered at the way in which the cure worked in the name of Jesus. Without medicine of any kind, Addai too healed in the name of Jesus. As for Abdu, the son of Abdu, who had been suffering from gout in his feet, he was also healed: he brought his feet near Addai, and he [Addai] placed his hand upon them and healed him; and he never suffered from the gout again. He also produced great cures in the city, and showed wonderful and powerful works.

Abgar said to him, "Now that everyone knows that by the power of Jesus Christ you perform all these wonderful works, and we are wondering at your works, I beg you to tell us about the life of Christ, how it was, and about His glorious power and those miracles which we have heard that He performed, which you have witnessed with the rest of your companions." Addai said to him, "I will not hesitate to declare this. For that is why I was sent

---

[15] With regard to the syntagm "for a long time," the temporal interval is not mentioned by Eusebius in his *Ecclesiastical History*. Moses of Khoren, on the other side, in his *History of Armenia*, Book II, Chapter 30, claims that Abgar suffered from an ailment which had struck him first in Persia, more than seven years earlier, and that no doctor had been able to cure it since then.

here, namely to speak and to teach everyone, who, just like you, is willing to believe. Tomorrow, assemble for me all the people in this city, so that I may seed in them the Word of Life by preaching before them about the coming of Christ, how it was, and about His glorious power, and about Him who sent Him, for what and how He sent Him, and about His power and wonderful works, and about the glorious mysteries of His coming, of which He spoke while He was in the world, and about the confidence of His preaching, how and for what He lowered Himself, and humbled His glorious divinity by taking a body, and was crucified and descended to the house of the dead, and smote the dividing wall, which had never been removed, and gave life to the dead by letting Himself be slain, and descended by Himself, and ascended with many to His glorious Father, with whom He was from eternity in one glorious divinity." And Abgar ordered that they should present Addai with silver and gold.

Addai said to him, "How could we receive anything which is not ours? For, look, that which was ours we have abandoned, as we were commanded by our Master to be without purses and satchels, and carrying crosses on our shoulders, we were commanded to preach His Gospel to the whole creation; so the whole creation felt and suffered because of His crucifixion, which was for us, for the salvation of all humans." And he told before King Abgar, and before his princes and nobles, and before Augustina, the mother of Abgar, and before Shalmath, the daughter of Meherdath, the wife of Abgar,[16] about the signs of our

[16] Moses of Khoren mentions that Helena, the first wife of Abgar, was a pious woman who had renounced idolatry. He also states that the tomb

Master and His wonders, and about the glorious miracles which He performed, and about His divine triumphs and ascension to His Father; and about how they received powers and abilities at the time He ascended, even as the power by which he had healed Abgar and Abdu, the son of Abdu, the second in authority over his kingdom; and about how he made them know that which would be revealed at the end of times, and in the demise of all creatures, and the revival and resurrection, which is to occur for all humans, and the separation which is to take place between the sheep and the goats, and between the faithful and the unbelieving. And he said to them, "Because the gate of life is strait and the way of truth is narrow, few are the believers of truth, and the power of unbelief is Satan's pastime. Because of this there are many liars, who cause to sin those who look on. For except that there is a good end for the faithful, our Master had not descended from heaven, and come to take birth, and to suffer death, and also He had not sent us to be His preachers and evangelists. Those things which we saw and heard from Him, things which He did and taught, we confidently preach before all; for we would not commit any transgression with respect to the truth of His Gospel. And not only these things, but those which were done in His name, after His ascension, we also show and preach.

I will tell all of you what happened and was done in the presence of those who, just like you, believed in Christ, namely that He is the Son of the living God. Protonice – the

---

of Helena, which in his day was to be seen before the gate of Jerusalem, was a very impressive one (*History of Armenia*, Book II, Chapter 35).

wife of the Emperor Claudius,[17] whom Tiberius made second[18] in his kingdom when he went to fight against the Hispaniards, who had waged war against him – saw the signs and wonders and marvellous works done in the name of Christ by Simon, one of the disciples, when he was in the city of Rome, and she denied the paganism of her forefathers in which she was brought up, and the idolatrous images which she had worshipped; and she believed in Christ our Master, and worshipped Him, and praised with those who were gathered around Simon, and held the Lord in great honour. After this, she also wished to see Jerusalem, and those places in which the mighty works of our Master were done. So she left without delay and descended from Rome to Jerusalem.

In Jerusalem, its dwellers went forth to meet her, and they received her with great honour, as a queen is due to be received, for she was the mistress of the great country of the Romans. But James, who was made principal and ruler in the church which was built for us there, when he had heard for what reason she had travelled to that remote place, arose and went to her. And he went to see her at her dwelling-place, in the great royal palace of King Herod. When she saw him, she received him with great joy, in the same way she had received Simon Peter. He also showed

---

[17] "L'Histoire detachée de la première invention de la Croix dit plus clairement que c'était Claude qui alla centre les Espagnols pendant que Tibere était absent de Rome. Cette guerre d'Espagne mentionnee ici et plus bas dans la lettre de Tibere a Abgar n'est citée par aucun auteur Romain: cependant il est très probable que notre auteur fait allusion aux intrigues et aux spoliations des biens des hommes les plus riches d'Espagne et de Gaule, faites par l'ordre de Tibère (v. Suétone, Tiber. 49; Tacite, *Annal*. vi. 19)." – *Lettre d'Abgar*, p. 19.

[18] Second in command.

her cures and powerful works, as those performed by Simon, and she said to him, 'Show me Golgotha, upon which Christ was crucified, and the wood of His cross upon which He was hung by the Jews, and the grave in which He was placed.'

James said to her, 'These three things your Majesty wishes to see are under the control of the Jews. They possess them, and do not allow us to go to pray there before Golgotha and the grave, and neither the wood of His cross will they give us. And not only this, but they also relentlessly harass us, so that we may not write and preach about Christ, and many times they put us in prison.'

When she heard these things, the queen without more ado commanded, and they brought before her Onias, the son of Hanan the priest, and Gedalia, the son of Caiaphas, and Judah, the son of Ebed Shalom, chiefs and leaders of the Jews. And she said to them, 'Give access to James and to those who are of the same mind with him to Golgotha, the grave, and the wood of the cross, and let no one forbid them to minister there according to the practice of their ministry.' And when she had so commanded the priests, she went to see those places; and she delivered those places to James and to those who accompanied him. After that, she entered the grave, and found therein three crosses, one of our Master, and two of those thieves who were crucified with Him, on His right hand and on His left. And at the time she and her children entered the grave, at that very instant her maiden daughter fell down and died, without pain, without disease, and without any cause of death. And when the queen saw that her daughter had unexpectedly died, she kneeled and prayed inside the grave, and said in her supplication, 'God, who gave Himself to death for all humans, and was crucified right in this place, and was laid in this grave; and as God who keeps everyone alive has risen and made many to rise with Him, let the Jews, the crucifiers, hear, along with the transgressing heathens, whose idols, carved images and terrors of paganism I have denied; make them not see me, deride me, and say that all which has happened to her is because she denied the gods that she had worshipped, having confessed Christ instead, whom she knew not, and went to honour the place of His grave and His crucifixion; and if, O my Master, I am not worthy to be heard, because I have worshipped idols instead of You, spare Yourself, for the sake of Your glorious name, so that it may not be blasphemed in this place, as they blasphemed You at Your crucifixion.' She said all these words in her prayer, and, in the exhilaration of her supplication, she repeated them before all those who were present.

Her eldest son approached her, saying to her, 'Hear what I have to say to your Majesty. I think thus in my mind that the death of my sister, which was unexpected, is not in vain; but it is in fact a wonderful work, according to which the name of God will be praised, not blasphemed. For, behold, we enter into the grave and find therein three crosses, and we know not which of them is the cross upon which Christ was hung. In the death of my sister, we may be able to see and learn which is the cross of Christ, for Christ never neglects those who believe in Him, and search for Him.'

Queen Protonice, who was very crestfallen at this time, saw in her mind that her son had uttered wise words, just and truthful. And with her own hands she took hold of one of the crosses and placed it on the dead body of her daughter, which lay before her, and prayed thus: 'O God who has shown wonderful works in this vey place, as we have heard and believed, if this cross, O Master, is Yours, and upon it Your humanhood was hung by the wicked, show the strong and almighty power of Your divinity, which rests in the humanhood, and bring back to life my daughter, so that she may arise, and Your name shall be glorified in her. May her soul revisit her body, so that Your crucifiers may be bewildered and Your worshippers may exult! And she waited a long time after she had such spoken. After that, she removed that cross from her daughter's dead body, placed another, and then said in her supplication: 'O God, by whose will worlds and creatures endure, wishing the life of all mortals that they may turn to Him, and is not forgetful of the prayers of those who seek Him, if this cross is Yours, O Master, show the power of Your triumphs as You always do, and bring back to life my daughter, so that she may arise, and thus the heathens, who worship Your creation instead of You, may be marvelled, and the faithful and the truthful may confess, so that their mouth may be opened to Your praise before those who reject You!' And she waited a long time after having said these things, and took the second cross from upon her daughter; and then she took the third cross and placed it on her daughter. Before she lifted her eyes to heaven and opened her mouth in prayer, at the time, at the very moment, which took less than the blinking of an eye, the cross touched the dead body of her daughter, she came back to life, and arose abruptly, giving praise to God, who had restored her to life by the power of His cross.

When she saw how her daughter came back to life, Queen Protonice trembled, and was greatly frightened; but, although frightened, she glorified Christ, and confessed Him, naming Him the Son of the living God. Her son said to her, 'My lady, you see that if this had not happened today, it might have occurred that they would have abandoned the cross of Christ, by which my sister came back to life, and might have taken and honoured one of those murderous thieves. Now, look, we have seen and may exult, and Christ, who has done this, may be glorified in her.'[19] And she took the cross of Christ, and gave it to James, so that it might be kept in the greatest honour. She also ordered that a great and marvellous building be erected over Golgotha, on which He was crucified, and over the grave in which He was placed, so that these places might be honoured and used for prayer and service.

When she saw all the inhabitants of that of the city, which she had assembled for the sight of this work, the queen ordered that her daughter walk without the covering of honour worn by the royals to the palace of the king wherein she resided, so that everyone could see her and give praise to God. But both Jewish people and gentiles, who rejoiced at the beginning of this happening and were

---

[19] The story of the finding of the cross is identical with that of its discovery by Helena, the mother of Constantine. According to the story, upon her arrival in Jerusalem, Helena gave orders for a Christian church to be built on Mount Calvary. In digging its foundation, a few pieces of wood were discovered, which were recognized as belonging to the cross on which Jesus had been crucified. These pieces were then sent by Helena to Constantine.

exultant, became very sad towards the end of it. For they would have been better pleased if this event had not occurred, for they noticed that, on account of this event, many began to believe in Christ; and especially when they noticed that the miracles done in His Name after His ascension were many more than those performed before His ascension.

The notoriety of this occurrence travelled to remote countries, and so did the message of the Apostles, my companions, who preached about Christ. And there was respite in the churches of Jerusalem, and in the cities around it; and both those who witnessed this occurrence and those who did not see it, praised God. And when the Queen returned from Jerusalem to Rome, the people of every city she entered flocked to take sight of her daughter. And when she had entered Rome, she told Emperor Claudius all the things that had happened; and when the Emperor heard that, he ordered that all Jews be banished from Rome.

Many people began to speak of that occurrence, and soon word of the deed travelled to Simon Peter. 'Whatever the Apostles, my companions, did, we preach before every person, so that those who do not know may also hear of those things which, by our hand, Christ did in the open, so that our Master might be glorified by every human being. The things which I repeat before you are told so that you may know and understand how great the faith of Christ is among those who truly embrace His message.'

James, the chief of the Church of Jerusalem, who also witnessed the deed, gave a written account, and sent it to the Apostles, my companions, in the cities of their countries. The Apostles themselves gave written accounts as well, and made known to James all that Christ had done by their hands, and these were read before every multitude of believers.

Upon hearing these things, Abgar the King and Augustina, his mother, and Shalmath, the daughter of Meherdath, and Phocreas, and Abdshemesh, and Shomshagrom, and Abdu, and Aghi and Bar Kalba, along with the rest of their companions, rejoiced tremendously and glorified God, and confessed Christ.

Abgar the King said to Addai, 'I wish that everything which we have heard from you today, and all the other things, you would tell overtly before all the inhabitants of this city, so that everyone may hear the preaching of the Gospel of Christ, which you teach to us, so that they may be firmly established in the doctrine which you teach to us, so that many may understand that I was in the right to believe in Christ, in the letter that I sent to Him, and may know that He is God, the Son of God, and you are His true and faithful disciple, and that you show His glorious power by performing miracles before all those who wish to believe in Him.'

The next day, Abgar commanded Abdu, the son of Abdu, who had been healed of a painful disease of his feet, to send a messenger in order to proclaim in all the city that the whole population must be assembled, men and women alike, at the place which was called Beththabara, the ample space of the house of Avida, the son of Abdnachad, so that they might hear the doctrine of Addai the Apostle, and how he taught about the One who gave him the power to cure and perform those miracles, wonders which he did incessantly. For when he healed Abgar the King, it was the nobles only who stood before him, and saw him when he healed him by the Word of Christ, whom many physicians had proven to be incapable of healing; and now a stranger cured him by the faith of Christ.

When all the dwellers of that city had been assembled, men and women alike, as the King had commanded, Avida and Labbu, and Chaphsai, and Bar Kalba, and Labubna, and Chesrun,[20] and Shomshagrom, they all stood there, with their companions, who were princes and nobles of the royal court, and various high officials; and there also were all the workmen and the artisans and the Jews and the Gentiles living in that city; and there were also foreigners from the countries of Soba and Harran, and the rest of the dwellers of all Mesopotamia; and all of them stood to hear the doctrine of Addai, about whom they had heard that he was the disciple of Jesus, who was crucified in Jerusalem, and he performed cures in His name. And Addai began to speak to them like this: "Hear, all of you, and understand that which I will speak before you; I am not a physician who uses medicines and roots, expert in the art of the sons of men; I am instead the disciple of Jesus Christ, the Physician of distressed souls, and the Saviour of future life, the Son of God, who descended from heaven, and was clad in a body and became a human being; and He gave Himself on the cross for all humanity. And when He was hung on the wooden cross, He darkened the sun in the sky; and when He entered the grave, He arose and, leaving the grave behind, went

---

[20] Moses of Khoren mentions Chesrun twice in Book II of his *History of Armenia*.

into view with many. And the guards of the grave did not see how He came out of the grave; yet, the angels of heaven were the preachers and writers of His resurrection; and if He had not wished, He would not have died, because He is the master of death, the way out of all things. And if it had pleased Him, He would not have again covered Himself with a body, for He is Himself the coverer of the body. For the will that predisposed Him to the birth from a virgin, also made Him lower Himself to the pangs of death, and He cancelled the magnificence of His illustrious divinity,[21] who was with His Father from the beginning of occurrence, He of whom the prophets of olden times spoke in their mysteries; and they illustrated him in signs of His birth, and His suffering, and His resurrection, and His ascension to His Father, and of His sitting at the right hand of the Father. And, look, He is worshipped by celestial beings, and by the dwellers of the earth, He who is worshipped since the beginning of time. For although He had the semblance of mortal men, His power, and His knowledge, and His command were of God Himself; as He said to us,[22] 'Behold, now is the son of man exalted, and God exalts Himself in Him, by miracles and by wonders, and by the honour of being at the right hand of the Father.' But His body is the pure vestment of His wonderful holiness, by which we are able to see His invisible command. Therefore, along Jesus Christ of whom we preach and write upon, we also praise His Father and the

---

[21] The word "divinity" is rarely used before the times of the Apostles, when Christianity becomes to some extent a sound theological system with a well-defined theological lexic.

[22] The words which immediately follow are very similar to those in John 13:31.

Spirit of His divinity, because that is what He commanded us, namely to baptize and forgive those who believe in the name of the Father and the Son and the Holy Spirit. The Prophets of the olden times spoke like this: 'The Lord God and His Spirit sent us.'[23] And if I articulate a word that was not spoken by the Prophets, the Jews, who are standing among you and hear me, will not receive it; and if, again, I say the name of Christ over those who have illnesses and diseases, and they are not healed by this wonderful name, they, who worship the work of their hands, will not believe.

So, if these things that we say are written in the books of the Prophets,[24] and we are capable of proving the healing powers over the sick, not a single person will look on us without discerning the faith that we preach, according to which God was crucified for all humanity. If there are those who do not wish to accept these words, let them come near us, and reveal to us what is on their mind, for if they suffer from an infirmity of the mind we may offer them healing medicine for the cure of their illness. For even though you were not present at the time of the agony of Christ, but you saw the darkened sun, learn and understand the great dismay there was at the time of the crucifixion of Him whose Gospel has spread all over the world, by the power of the wonderful works that His disciples, my companions, are performing all over the earth. And those who were Jewish, and knew only the Hebrew language, as taught by their mothers, look, today they can speak in all

[23] This passage is from Isaiah 18:16. The only variation is the change of the plural pronoun "us" into "me." This is evidently due to the fact that Addai uses the so-called "plural of authority."

[24] This passage does not appear in the Syriac text.

languages, so that both those who dwell in distant lands and those who do not can hear and believe that He is the same, He who confused the tongues[25] of the wicked in this region which lies before us; it is He who today teaches the meek and the desolate from Galilee in Israel through us the faith of truth and genuineness. I, whom you can see, am also from Paneas,[26] from where the Jordan River springs. And I was chosen, along with my companions, to be a preacher of this Gospel, by which, look, every region resonates with the wonderful name of the worshippable Christ. Let for that reason none of you possess a heavy heart against the truth and keep their minds at a distance from truthfulness. Do not be led by thoughts destructively sinful, which are full of the anguish of a miserable death.[27] Do not be led astray by the evil customs of your heathen forefathers that might keep you at a distance from the path of truthfulness, which is in Christ. For those who believe in Him are those who are trusted by Him, who willingly descended to us, to put an end to all the sacrifices made by the world's heathens, and to the offerings of idolatry, for those creatures should no longer be adored; but we should worship Him and His Father instead, and His Holy Spirit. For I, as my Master has commanded me, look, I preach and I write. And His silver coin, look, I throw before you on the table, and the seed of His word I sow in the ears of every person. Those who wish to receive it will also receive the good reward of

---

[25] Obviously, a reference to the confusion of the languages that occurred in Senaar, Babylonia, where the tower of Babel was built and where Noah settled after the flood, according to the Old Testament.

[26] The same as Caesarea Philippi.

[27] In the sense that one should not be led by the sinful thought that one can be able to escape death in this world.

confession; and those refusing to obey, against them I spread the dust of my feet, as my Master has commanded me. Therefore, my beloved, turn away from wicked ways and vile deeds; and turn to Him with a good and honest will, as He turned Himself to you with His mercy and His forgiving grace. And do not be as the bygone generations of olden times, who, because they hardened their heart against the fear of God, were punished plainly, being chastised in such a way that those who came after them could tremble with fear. Because that for which our Master came into the world was in fact[28] to teach and show that at the end of life there is a resurrection for all people. And at that time, their deeds will stand for their own persons, and their bodies will become books for the written things of justice, and there will not be anyone who does not know writing; for everyone will read the letters of his own book on that day, and the account of his actions he takes with the fingers of his hands. Therefore, the illiterate will know the new writing of the new language, and there is not one who will say to his fellow, 'Read this to me,' because over all people will reign one doctrine and one teaching.

Bear this thought in mind then, be vigilant, and open up your eyes, because if it passes from your mind, it cannot pass from His judgement.[29] Seek the mercy of God, so that He may forgive the detestable faithlessness of your heathenism, for you have abandoned Him who created you on this face of the earth, and makes His rain come down and His sun rise upon you, and you worship, instead of Him, His works. For, regarding the idols and heathen

---

[28] Or "entirely."

[29] Or "justice," which in Syriac has the same meaning as "judgement."

sculpted images, and whatever of the creation in which you believe and which you worship, if there were in them feeling and understanding, for the sake of which you worship and glorify them, it would be right for those things, which you have made and engraved, and have firmly fixed with nails so that they will not fall, to receive your honours. For if those creatures were aware of your worship, they would cry, yelling at you not to worship your fellow human beings who, even as yourselves, are made and created; because creatures that are made should not be worshipped; but that they should worship their Creator, and they should honour Him who created them. And, as His mercy is also meant for the sinful assembled here,[30] even so His justice shall eventually be avenged on the pagans abiding here. For I noticed that this very city has a great number of heathens among its dwellers, which is against the Word of God. Who is this Nebo,[31] an idol made which you worship, and Bel,[32] which you adore? For, look, there are those among you

[30] The word "here" has a soteriological connotation, as in the expression "here and there," wherein by "here" one should understand *this world* and by "there" *the world to come.*

[31] Nebo was a Babylonian idol. A reference to this deity is noticeable in the proper names Nebuchadnezzar and Nebuzaradan. Nebo was also worshipped in other places. For example, in Isaiah 46:1we read, "Bel boweth down, Nebo stoopeth, their idols were upon the beasts, and upon the cattle: your carriages were heavy loaden; they are a burden to the weary beast." It is believed that a temple dedicated to Nebo also existed in Dibon, a city of Moab.

[32] Bel was a Babylonian idol. While little is known of Bel, it seems that his worshippers attributed to him the gift of healing diseases. We also know that the Babylonians offered him food and water as a ritualistic sacrifice. See also the previous note.

who worship Bath Nical,[33] even as your neighbours, the inhabitants of Harran, and Taratha,[34] as the dwellers of Mabug, and the eagle, as the Arabs, and also the sun and the moon, as the rest of the population of Harran, who are just like yourselves. Be not led astray by the glow of the luminaries and the dazzling star; for everyone who worships creatures is doomed in the eyes of God. For although there are in the creation people who are greater than their fellow human beings, still they are fellow-servants of their fellow humans, as I have already explained to you. For this is a great suffering, for which there is no remedy, namely that things of the creation should worship things of the creation, and humans should glorify their fellow human beings. For as they are not able to stand by their own power, but by the power of Him who made them, even so they are not able to be honoured with Him, nor to be glorified with Him; for it is a blasphemy against both parties, against the creatures when they are honoured, and against the Creator, when the creatures, who do not know the nature of His being, are made partakers with Him.

---

[33] It is here stated that this goddess was worshipped in Harran. There is otherwise hardly any reliable information on Bath Nical. In the *History of Armenia*, Moses of Khoren calls this deity Pathincagh.

[34] Taratha, or Atargatis as she was also called, was considered by some – *e.g.*, Jacob of Serug in Assemani, *Bibliotheca Orient.* I. p. 327 – to be a correlative of Dagon. Others claimed that she was one with the goddess Derceto who was worshipped at Askelon under the shape of a woman with the lower parts of a fish. Assemani, in a note at the foot of the page cited above, says: "Tarata, Janus fortasse Syrorum nam Tara est Janua, unde faemininum Tarata, quod faeminae specie illud idolum colerent." See the discourse of Jacob of Serug on the fall of the idols published by M. l'Abbé Martin in the *Zeitschrift* of the German Oriental Society, note and translation, p. 131, for the year 1875. Moses of Khoren in his *History of Armenia* mentions four major deities, *i.e.*, Nabogus, Belus, Bathnicalus and Tharatha.

Truly, all the prophecy of the Prophets, and the preaching of us, who came after the Prophets, is this: creatures must not be worshipped along the Creator, and humans must not fasten themselves to the yoke of heathenism, which is fraudulent. It is not due to the creatures that one can see, I say, that they must not be honoured; but everything that is created is a creature, whether visible or not. It is indeed an awful impiety to place the wonderful name of God upon it. For it is not creatures, like you, that we proclaim and honour, but the Master of all creatures. The earthquake that made them tremble at the crucifixion testifies that everything which is created is dependent on and exists by the power of its Creator, who existed before worlds and creatures, whose nature is impenetrable and invisible, and, with His Father, is glorified in the heavens, for He is Master and God from the beginning of time. This is the doctrine that we preach in every country and in every region. For thus have we been commanded to preach to those who want to hear us, not by force, but by the teaching of truthfulness and by the power of the Lord. And the miracles which were worked in His name testify about our faith, namely that it is true and should be believed. Therefore, trust my words and receive that which I have said and am saying to you; and that I may not require your death, behold, I warn you to be very cautious. Receive my words properly, and do not ignore this teaching. Come near and listen to my words, you, those who are still far from Christ, and stand near Him. And instead of the wrong sacrifice and obeisance, offer now to Him the sacrifice of thanksgiving.

Whom is this great altar built by you in the centre of this city for? And what are those going back and forth, offering on it to demons, and sacrificing on it to devils? But if you do not know the Scriptures, does not nature itself teach you, by its power of sight, that your idols have eyes that cannot see? And you, who see with eyes which do not understand, you are also as they who can neither see, nor hear, and in vain you stimulate your voices, for they are useless to deaf ears. They are not to be blamed for that which they cannot hear, for by nature they are mute and deaf. And the fault with which righteousness is involved is yours, for you do not wish to understand, even that which you can see. Truly, the dense darkness of transgression, which is spread over your minds, does not let you perceive the heavenly light, which is the understanding of knowledge. Abandon, therefore, all things made and created, as I have informed you, that in name only are they called gods, for in their nature they are not truly gods; and approach Him who in His nature is God from ever and for ever, since He is not made, like your idols, nor is He a creature and a work of art as the images which you boast. Because even though He put on this mortal body, He was God along His Father; for the created nature, which shook when He was crucified, and was frightened by the agony of His death, was his work – that is what they testify. For it was not for a human being that the earth trembled, but for Him who established the earth upon the waters; and it was not for a human that the sun darkened in the skies, but for Him who made the majestic firmament. And it was not by a human being that the righteous and the just were brought to life again, but by Him who had been given authority over death from the beginning. Nor was it by a human the veil of the temple of the Jews that was rent from the top to the bottom, but by Him who said to them, 'Look, your house is left vacant.'[35] For, look, except they who crucified Him knew that He was the Son of God, they would not have proclaimed the vacancy of their city, nor would they have proscribed themselves. Even if they wished to overlook this confession, the awful mayhem which was at that time would not have allowed them. Look, some of the children of those who crucified Him have also become this day preachers and evangelists, with the Apostles, my companions, in all the land of Israel and among the Samaritans, and in all the country of the Philistines. The idols of heathenism are reviled, but the Cross of Christ is honoured. Peoples and creatures confess God, who became flesh. If, truthfully, when Jesus our Master was on earth you believed in Him that He is the Son of God, and before you had heard the word of His preaching, confessed that He is God, now that He has ascended to His Father, and you have seen the signs and miracles worked in His name, and the word of His Gospel you have heard with your ears, not a single one of you should doubt how the promise of His blessing that He sent to you would have been established with you: 'Blessed are you who have believed in Me, even though you have not seen Me; and since you have so believed in Me, the city in which you dwell will be blessed, and the enemies will never conquer it.'[36] Do not then turn

[35] *Cf.* Matth. XXXIII, p. 38.

[36] This is a quotation from the message of Jesus to Abgar. According to this passage, Urha became free from hostile invasion as a result of the blessing bestowed upon it by God.

from His faith; for, look, you have heard and seen those things which bear witness to His faith, namely that He is the worshippable Son, and the glorious God, and the victorious King, and the Omnipotent Power; and by His true faith one can acquire the true mind's eye and understand that if one honours creatures, this same one will be crushed by the wrath of righteousness.

Verily, everything that we say here in front of you, we say as a gift which we have received from our Master; and we teach and show how to have power over your life, and not destroy your spirits by the fault of heathenism; because the light of heaven has already risen upon creation, and it is He who has chosen the ancient fathers and the righteous people and the Prophets, and has spoken with them by the revelation of the Holy Spirit. For He is the God of the Jews, who have crucified Him, and the mistaken Gentiles also worship Him, even though they have no knowledge of it; because there is no other god in heaven and on earth; and, look, confession in Him ascends to Him from the four corners of the world. Look, your ears have now heard that which was not heard before by you; and behold, again, for your eyes have seen that which was never seen before by you. Be therefore just to that which you have heard and seen. Reject the rebellious thoughts of your fathers, and free yourselves from the yoke of transgression, which has power over you by libations and sacrifices made before sculpted images. Let it be a warning to you regarding your soon-to-end lives, and regarding your vain obeisance, and obtain the new mind which glorifies the Maker and not the thing made, in which is represented the image of truth and actuality of the Father, and of the

Son, and of the Holy Spirit, when you believe and are baptized in the glorious names of the Trinity. This is our doctrine and preaching! For it is not in many that the truth of Christ is celebrated. So those of you who are willing to be obedient to Christ, know that I have repeated my words before you many times, so that you might learn and understand what your ears hear. And we will exult in this, even as the worker in his field which is blessed; for our God is glorified by your repentance in Him. And as you live in this, we who guide you thus will also be blessed and rewarded. And because I am certain that you dwell in a blessed land, according to the will of our Master Christ, because the dust of my feet which we have been commanded[37] to shake off against the city that refuses to receive our words, look, I shake off today at the door of your ears by the power of the words of my lips, which speak of the coming of Christ, that which has already occurred and that which has not yet occurred, and the awaking and resurrection of all people, and the separation which is to be made between the faithful and the faithless, and the blessed promise of future delights which they who have believed in Christ and worshipped His Great Father, and confessed Him and the Spirit of His Godhead, will be given. And now it is time for us to finish our preaching, and let those who have received the word of Christ remain with us and join us in prayer if they will, and then let them go to their homes."

Addai the Apostle was much gladdened by that city's multitudes, who chose to remain with him; as for those who did not remain at that time, they were few; and

---

[37] *Cf.* Matth. X, p. 14.

these same few, after several days, received his words and confessed the gospel of the preaching of Christ. And when Addai the Apostle had said these things before all the city of Urha, and King Abgar saw that all the city rejoiced in his doctrine, men and women alike, and were saying to him, "Christ, who has sent you to us is true and trustworthy," he also greatly rejoiced in this, glorifying God, that according to what he had heard from Hanan, the keeper of the royal archives, regarding Christ, so he had seen the wonderful mighty works which Addai the Apostle had performed in the name of Christ. And King Abgar also said to Addai the Apostle, "As I sent my letter to Christ, and as He also answered me through you this very day, so will I believe all the days of my life, and in the same things persist, glorifying God, because I know that there is no other power in the name of whom these signs and wonders are done, but by the power of Christ alone, whom you preach in truth and honestly. And now I will worship Him, I and Manu,[38] my son, and Augustina, and Shalmath, my queen. So now, wherever you wish, build a church, a house of assembly for those who have believed, and will continue to believe in your words. And, as instructed by your Master, minister you at times with assurance. And to those who teach with you this Gospel, I am ready to offer them significant gifts, so that they may not have any worries with the ministry. Anything else that you require for the expenses of the house, I will give you without taking account; your word will be potent and have authority in this city, and without

[38] The name of Abgar's father was Ma'nu as well. Ma'nu was also the name of other kings of Urha.

the need to respond to any guard, you will have power to enter into my presence in my royal palace of honour."

When King Abgar descended to his royal palace, he rejoiced along his princes – Abdu, Garmai, Shomshagrom, Abubai, and Meherdath – and the rest of their companions, at everything their eyes could see and their ears could hear, and in the joy of their hearts they praised God, who had turned their minds to Him. They renounced the heathenism in which they had stood, and confessed the Gospel of Christ. And when Addai built a church, they offered in it vows and offerings, and there they and the people of the city worshipped all the remaining days of their lives.

Avida and Barkalba, two chiefs and rulers whose heads were adorned with royal bands, approached Addai and asked him about the history of Christ; they wished to know how He could be seen by them both as God and man, and how he saw Him. And he satisfied them their interest, concerning all which their eyes had seen, and concerning all which their ears had heard of Him. And everything which the Prophets had said about Him, he repeated before them, and they received his words cheerfully and devotedly, and there was not a single soul who stood up against him. For the wonderful works which he performed did not permit a single soul to stand up against him.

Then, Shavida and Ebednebo, the chief-priests of this city, and their companions Piroz[39] and Diku, when they saw the wonders which he worked, ran and broke down all the altars upon which they sacrificed before their gods Nebo and Bel, except the great altar, which was in the centre of the city; and they cried out and said that this was

---

[39] Probably the same name as that of Berosus.

indeed the disciple of the illustrious and glorious Master of whom they heard all those things which He did in the land of Israel. And Addai received all those who believed in Christ, and baptized them in the name of the Father, the Son, and the Holy Spirit. And those who had gotten accustomed to worshipping stones and animals, sat at his feet learning and being advised of the plague of the imprudence of heathenism. The Jews also, conversant with the Law and the Prophets, who carried on merchandise in silks,[40] were preached to and they became disciples, and made confession in Christ, that He is the Son of the living God. But neither King Abgar nor Addai the Apostle forced any person to believe in Christ; for it was not the force of a human being, but the force of the miracles that compelled many to believe in Him. And the entire region of Mesopotamia and all the provinces around it received his doctrine with devotion.

Aggai, who tailored the silk[41] vestments and made the headbands of the king, Palut, Barshelama and Barsamya with the rest of the other companions went to join Addai the Apostle, and he received them and made them members of his ministry. They read every day from the Old Testament[42] and from the New Testament, and from the

---

[40] In Luke 7:25 we have the same word rendered by “soft raiment.” See also Matthew 11:8. It is probable from what is said herein and referred to by other writers that the Jews of Urha traded silk from the Far East.

[41] Another possible translation is “chains.” Moses of Khoren, however, uses “silks.” Nonetheless, in Numbers 31:50 and Isaiah 3:22 only “silk” suits the context.

[42] Since the Books of the Prophets are mentioned independently, the Old Testament here probably means just the Pentateuch. Similarly, as the Acts of the Apostles are named apart from the New Testament, the latter most likely refers to the Gospels only.

Prophets, and from the Acts of the Apostles, and they meditated on what they had read. He advised them wisely, "Let your bodies be pure, and let your persons be holy, for so it is right for the men who stand before the altar of God; and be truly far removed from false swearing, and from wicked killing, and from false testimony, which is one with adultery, and from sorcerers with respect to whom there is no forgiveness, and from divination, and soothsaying, and necromancy, and from fates, and nativities, which the errant Chaldees claim to master; and from stars, and the zodiacal signs, in which only the foolish confide. Keep away from sinful hypocrisy, bribes, and gifts, by which the pure are damned. And taking care of the ministry to which you have been called, let there not be for you another work; for the Lord Himself is the work of your ministry all the days of your life. Be also assiduous in offering the sign of baptism, and love not the gains of this world, but do justice in the spirit of fairness and truthfulness. And do not be a stumbling block to the blind, so that the name of He who opened the eyes of the blind, as we have seen, be not blasphemed through your deeds. Let all, then, who see you, notice that you perform all that you preach and instruct."

They preached with him in the church founded by Addai at the order of King Abgar. They were supported from the fortunes of the king and his nobles; and some of them gave for the house of God, and some for the feeding of the poor. And a large mass of people assembled on a daily basis, attending the service, praying conferences, and the readings from the Old Testament, New Testament, and

Diatessaron;[43] and since they believed in the resurrection of the dead, they buried their dead in the hope of the resurrection. They also observed the festivals of the Church in their times, and every day they were unvarying in the vigils of the Church, and they also performed charitable acts both to the sick and the needy, according to the teaching of Addai. And in various places around the city churches were built, and many received from him the hand of the priesthood. And many people from the east, with the appearance of merchants, came to the country of the Romans to see the works which Addai performed, and those of them who became disciples received from them the hand of the priesthood, and in their own country of Assyria they taught the sons of their people, and built there houses of prayer, but in secret, because of the danger arising from the fire and water worshippers.

However, Nersai,[44] the king of the Assyrians, when he heard of the signs which Addai the Apostle had done, he sent word to King Abgar: "Either send me the man who has performed these works with you, so that I may see him and hear his preaching, or send me an account of all the signs that you have seen him do in your city." And Abgar sent an

---

[43] The Diatessaron was compiled by Tatian, and was, as it appears from various secondary sources, in general use in the Syrian churches in the 2nd century AD. The Diatessaron was a volume compiled from the Four Gospels, and seems to have been publicly read at Urha until the 4th century. A commentary was written on this work by Ephraim Syrus, according to what is affirmed by Barsalibe and Bar Hebraeus, as the former says that Ephraim added commentaries to the Diatessaron, while the latter, in speaking of Tatian's volume, states that the meaning of the words with which the Gospel of John opens, "In the beginning was the Word," was explicated by Ephraim.

[44] Moses of Khoren refers to this king in his *History of Armenia* as "the young Nerseh."

epistle to Nersai and made him familiar with the entire story of the works of Addai, from the beginning to the end, leaving no detail unmentioned in the letter.

When Nersai read the things that had been written to him, he wondered and was amazed. But King Abgar, because he was not able to enter the country of the Romans in order to travel to Israel and slay the Jews, as punishment for having crucified Christ, composed a letter and sent it to Emperor Tiberius, writing in it the following: "Abgar the King to our Master Emperor Tiberius, Peaceful greetings! Knowing that nothing is secreted from your majesty, I write to inform your awe-inspiring and great sovereignty that the Jews, who are under your dominion, and who dwell in the land of Israel, assembled together and crucified the Christ without any fault worthy of death, when he was doing before them signs and miracles, and showed them great works and wonderful things, so that He even raised the dead to life for them. And when they crucified Him, the sun became dark and the whole earth shook, and all creatures trembled, and as though of themselves, all kinds of creatures were frightened upon seeing this, and so were all human beings. And now your majesty knows what is just to decree against the Jews, who did these things."

Emperor Tiberius wrote an epistle and sent it to King Abgar, letting him know the following: "I have received the letter of your loyalty to me, which was read entirely to me. Regarding that which the Jews have done with the cross, Pilate the governor has also written, and informed Olbinus,[45] my proconsul, of all these things that

[45] Since no person by the name of Olbinus was governor of Judaea at the time mentioned in the document, most likely that that this name has

you have written me. Nevertheless, because of the war with the Hispaniards who have rebelled against me, which is occurring at this very time, I have not been able to punish them for this matter; but I am prepared, when I have attained peace, to indict the Jews, who have not acted legally. As for Pilate, whom I made the governor there, I have sent another in his place because of this, and I have dismissed him with dishonour, for he defied the law and did the will of the Jews, and he crucified Christ to satisfy the Jews, who, in accordance with that which I have heard about them, instead of placing Him on the cross of death, they should have honoured Him, for He deserved to be worshipped by them, especially as they witnessed all the works that He did. But you, based on your loyalty to me and your true agreement and that of your forefathers, have done well to write to me about all this."

Then King Abgar received Artidias, who had been sent to him by Emperor Tiberius, and he replied that he sent him back with expensive gifts, which were worthy of the one who sent him his guest. And he left Urha, heading for Ticnutha,[46] where Claudius the Second was, and from there he also went on to Artica, where Emperor Tiberius was at the time. And Gaius safeguarded the region where the Emperor was. Artidias himself also recounted before Emperor Tiberius the great works which Addai performed before King Abgar. And when the war duties permitted it, he sent some of his soldiers to Israel, to slay a few of the chiefs of the Jews. And when King Abgar heard of this

---

been confused with that of Albinus, whom Nero made governor of Judaea in A.D. 62. This could be an error made by the original editor of the manuscript.

[46] According to other sources, Thicnutha or Nuthicontha.

deed, he greatly rejoiced at this, knowing that the Jews had been chastised, having received what they deserved.

A few years after Addai the Apostle had built the church in Urha and furnished it with everything that was appropriate for it, and had taught many people of the city and of the villages, both distant and nearby, he began to build churches, and when he completed them, he started to enrich them with adornments; he also appointed deacons and elders, and preached in them to those who should read the Scriptures, and instructed the orders of the ministry both inside and outside.

After having performed all these things, Addai the Apostle conceived the thought of visiting the countries of the East and Assyria in order to preach there, but he was struck by the illness which would take him from this world.[47] But prior to that, he called Aggai before all the congregation of the church and, bringing him near, made him governor and ruler in his place. As for Palut, who was a deacon, he made him an elder, while Barshelama, who was a scribe, he made a deacon. And when the aristocrats and chiefs were assembled and stood by him, Bar Kalba, son of Zati,[48] and Bar-Zati, and Marihab, the son of Barshemesh, and Sennac, son of Avida, and Peroz, son of Patricius, with the rest of the cohort, Addai the Apostle said to them:

"You know, and you bear witness, all of you who hear me, that everything I have preached to you and

---

[47] Here the Armenian text and the Syriac one differ greatly. In the latter it is said that Addai had assembled around him the nobles and chiefs to deliver to them his farewell speech.

[48] The Syriac text reads "Bar-Kalba, and Bar-Zati" instead of "Bar Kalba, son of Zati."

instructed you, and you have heard from me, I have also followed myself among you, and you have seen that in my works, for that is what our Master has commanded us, namely that whatever we preach in words before the people, we should also do before every person. And according to the laws and edicts which were decreed in Jerusalem, and by which the Apostles, my companions, were also governed, you must neither turn away from them, nor leave out anything from them, as I too have been guided by them among you, and have not turned away from them to the right hand, or to the left, that I might not stray from the promised salvation, which awaits those who are steered by them. Take heed, thus, to this ministry which you hold, and abide in it with fear and in awe, and minister every day. But do not minister by habits that bring disdain; minister instead with the forethought of faith; as for the praises of Christ, never let them cease from your mouth, and do not permit lassitude in prayer at the fixed times overwhelm you. Hold to the truth, which you have known, and to the teaching of the truth, which you have been given, and to the legacy of salvation, which I entrust to you, since you will be summoned before the judgment throne of Christ by Him, when He takes account with the ministers and elders, and when He takes His money from merchants with the boost of profits. For He is the King's Son, and went to receive a kingdom, and shall return to resurrect all humans; and then He shall sit on the throne of justice, and judge the dead and the living, as He has promised us. Do not let your mind's hidden eye from the height above be closed, so that your transgressions may not increase in the way in which you start to think that your monstrous offences are not even transgressions.

Find those who are lost, and seek those who sin, and rejoice in those who are corrected. Bind up those who are aching, and watch the lambs carefully, for the sheep of Christ will be in your own hands. Do not look to vainglory, for the shepherd who seeks to be honoured by his flock will herd his flock truly badly. Let your consideration for the young lambs be great, for their angels[49] look at the face of the unseen Father; and do not be a stumbling stone before the blind, but clearers[50] of the way and the path in a difficult spot of land, among the Jews, the crucifiers, and the mistaken pagans; for even with only these two sides, there is already war for you, in order to confirm the truth of the faith that you hold; also when you are silent, your humble and honourable appearance will be your weapon against those who loathe truthfulness and love untruth. Do not put down the poor before the rich, for the stern suffering of their poverty is already too much for them. Be not tempted by the odious schemes of Satan, so that you may not be stripped naked of the faith that you have put on, for non-belief is easier than faith, even as sin is easier than virtue. Pay attention, therefore, to those who crucified Him, and do not make friends with them, so that you will not be held accountable along those whose hands are tainted by the blood of Christ; so know, and keep in mind that everything we say and teach about the life and deeds of Christ is written in the Book of the Prophets, and placed with them. And their words bear witness to our teachings

---

[49] See Matthew 18:10.

[50] Literally, "cleansers of the way."

about the trial, agony, resurrection, and ascension of Christ; but they do not know that when they rise against us, they rise against the words of the Prophets, and as they persecuted the Prophets in the past, so do they now, because ever since the day they [the Prophets] died, they persecuted the truth, which is written in the Book of the Prophets.

Beware of the pagans too, for they worship the sun and the moon, and Bel and Nebo, and the rest of those which they call gods, even though they are not gods in their nature. Run away, therefore, from them, for they worship creatures and things made by human hands. And as I said to you before, the main purpose[51] for which our Master came into the world was that creatures might not again be worshipped and glorified, because they exist by the approval of their Creator; and when He wills, He destroys them and makes them disappear, and they are as if they were not. For the will of He who made all creatures, has freed human beings from the yoke of the heathenism of the creatures. For you know that those who honour the servants of a king together with the king will find in their worship their own death by the sword. Do not search for hidden things, and do not inquire after secret things, which are written in your holy books. Do not establish judgement over the words of the Prophets. Remember and reflect that they are said by the Spirit of God; and he who lays blame on the Prophets lays blame on the Spirit of God. May we refrain from that, for the ways of the Master are straight,

[51]Earlier we learned from the same text that the reason Jesus came into this world was to teach about the resurrection of all humanity. Here, however, it is stated that the purpose for which Jesus came into the world was to forbid the worshipping of creatures.

and the virtuous walk on them is without stumbling: only the unbelievers stumble on them; because they do not possess the secret eye of the secret mind, which has no need of questions that bring no profit, but only loss.[52] Remember that by establishing judgment over the Prophets and over the Word of our Master, which has created all words, including yours, the Master will judge you by fire, and all people will be tried by it. For that reason, consider yourselves to be no more than travellers and sojourners who tarry for a night before returning early to their homes – think that from here you shall go forth to the place where the Son went to prepare a dwelling for every one of you. As in the case of kings, whose armies go forth before them, and set up for them a dwelling-place of honour; as for our King, look, He has gone to prepare for those who believe in Him consecrated mansions[53] so that they may dwell therein. For God did not create the children of men in vain; but to worship and glorify Him, both here and in the hereafter. As He has eternal life, so shall have those who do not cease worshipping Him. As for my near death, which will be the result of the affliction that has bound me to my bed, consider it just a night's sleep, and let it be well-regarded in your eyes. And remember that with the torment of the Son, death, which had snatched away the children of humankind, passed away for good; and Satan, who causes many to err and struggles with truthfulness, so that they may be in the wrong, is as if dead. And like a husband who ploughs the land and, looking back,[54] sees that the furrows

[52] They waste their time in futile debates.
[53] See John 14:2.
[54] See Luke 9:62.

are not straight, so also you who have been called to this gift of the ministry: be watchful therefore, so that you do not trouble yourselves with the things of this world, lest inadvertently you be hindered as to that to which you have been called.

As to the great men and judges who have embraced this faith, love them, but with a truthful heart, and if they sin, rebuke them, but with justice. Show them plainly your righteousness, so that they may be corrected: in this way, they will never again conduct themselves after their own accord. This concern you must have as long as you live, so that all of you may seek only what is honest, as you also advise others in respect to them; it is in these things that people find their life before God.

As for the Law,[55] and the Prophets, and the Gospel, which you read every day before the people, and the Epistles of Paul, which Simon Peter sent us from the city of Rome, and the Acts of the twelve Apostles, which John, the son of Zebedee, sent us from Ephesus, read these books in the churches of Christ, but no others besides these, for the truth that you hold is not written in any other book; only these books shall keep you in the faith to which you have been called. And our master King Abgar, and his honoured court, who have heard that which I have spoken before you today are adequate witnesses for me after my passing, in order to confess that I have thoroughly preached the teachings of our Master before everyone, and that I have not acquired any material goods in this world by making

[55] The Holy Scriptures are more particularly enumerated here. The New Testament is described as consisting of the Gospel, the Epistles of Paul and the Acts of the Apostles. The two latter were probably not written at the time Addai was preaching Christianity in Urha.

use of His Word. For His Word, by which I have become satisfied was plenty for me, and I have made many rich by preaching it to them; for it raises me so that I go forth before Christ, who has sent after me, and thus, by it, I will have the power to go to Him. For you know that which I have said to you, "That all souls which depart from this body, do not perish; but they will live and ascend, and have mansions, and an abode for rest, since the understanding and acumen of the soul do not cease, because the image of God is reflected in it, and therefore it does not die. For the soul is not like the body, that is, without feeling: for the body does not perceive the horrible corruption that has come upon it. And the soul is unable to receive any reward and recompense without the body. Because the labour for that prize is not solely its own, but also that of the body in which it lived. But the disobedient who do not know God become penitent then to no avail. You, truly, who are of Christ, whose wonderful name dwells in your heart, and is its ruler, He will direct you in the way of truth, in which you will travel and will disembark and attain to that which is promised and kept for those who do not stray Him from his path, but live instead according to what they have been called to by our Master."

The moment Addai the Apostle had finished his teaching, he fell silent. And Aggai, maker of the king's vestments, and Palut, and Barshelama, with the rest of their companions, answered in this way to Addai the Apostle, "Christ Himself has testified that He sent you to us, and you have taught us the true faith, and have made us obtain the true life. As we have heard from you and received so much, and all this time you have been with us, so that we can enjoy each day of our lives. And from the adoration of things made and created, which our fathers worshipped, we turn around, and from the Jews, the crucifiers, we will stand away; and this legacy, which we have received from you, we shall not let go, but with it we shall leave this world. And in the day of our Master, before the judgment-throne of uprightness, there will He return to us this legacy as that of which you have spoken to us."

When he finished speaking, King Abgar stood up, and so did the princes, and all the nobles of his court, and he went to his own palace; and all of them grieved over him, for he was at death's door. And he sent him admirable and precious garments, in which to be buried; and when Addai saw them, he sent word to him, informing him that he had never taken anything from him, and he was not willing to falsify in him the Word of Christ, who said to him, "Do not receive anything from human beings, and do not acquire anything in this world."[56] And three days after Addai the Apostle had said these things and he had heard and received the testimony of the doctrine of his teaching from the sons of his ministry before all the nobles, he left this world: it was the fifth day of the week, on the fourteenth day of the month of May.[57] And the whole city

---

[56] Even though these words are not according to the epistle, they are obviously in the spirit of the instructions which Jesus delivered to the twelve disciples at their ordination, since we find them in Matthew 10:7-10.

[57] In Assemani, *Bibl. Orient*. Vol II, p. 392 we read that Bar Hebraeus affirmed "that Addai the Apostle was slain on the 30th of July, and buried in the church, which he himself had built in Urha." This date, however, is contradicted by a footnote on the same page, from which we learn that "Amrus Matthaei filius historicus Nestorianus, qui Chronicon Maris ejusdem sectae scriptoris in compendium redegit,

was in great distress and bitter pain; not only Christians mourned Him, but also the Jews and heathens who dwelt in that city.

King Abgar and his sons mourned him more than anyone in the kingdom. And in the grief of his mind, Abgar loathed and abandoned the honour of his royalty on that day, and with woeful tears he wept over him like an ordinary citizen. And all the people of the city, when they saw him, wondered at how much he suffered because of his death. And with great and outstanding honour he carried him to the burial place, as though he were of royal status, and he placed him in a beautifully sculpted tomb, in which those of the dynasty of Aryu, the ancestors of the father of King Abgar, had been laid to rest. There he placed him gently with grief and great distress. And all the members of the congregation went to his tomb from time to time, and prayed there arduously, and the memorial of his death they observed every year, according to the command and teaching received by them from Addai the Apostle, and according to the word of Aggai, who was now the guide and head of the church, invested by the hand of the priesthood, which he had received from him in front of everyone.

At this time Aggai, by the same hand from which he had received the gift of priesthood, made priests and chiefs in all the region of Mesopotamia. For they too, even as Addai the Apostle, took his word and heard and received, considering him a true and faithful heir of the Apostle of

---

Addaeum obiise refert, non die 30 Julii, sed 14 Maii. Et quidem in pervetusto Kalendario Syriaco, quod ad calcem Codicis 32 in fine hujus tomi subjicitur, die Maii 14, Addaeus decessisse dicitur."

the worshippable Christ. He, however, did not take gold and silver from anyone, and the gifts of the princes he refused. For he enriched the Church of Christ with the souls of the faithful, not with gold and silver. And all the chiefs[58] of men and women were modest and well-behaved, and holy and pure, and they lived by themselves and unassumingly without blemish, in decent vigilance of the ministry, taking care of the sick and poor; and their acts were full of the praise of all those who saw them, and their words were honoured by the strangers who met them; so that even the priests of the temple of Nebo and Bel glorified them at all times, because of their honourable aspect, truthful discourse, the self-reliance which they possessed, and their freedom, which was not the slave of avarice, and was not spotted by any guilt. For all those who saw them were eager to meet them and greet them with great honour; for even the sight of them veiled one in much composure. For their words of peace were spread like nets over the unruly, when they were entering the fortress of truth and certainty. For there was no human being who saw them, and was embarrassed by them; because they performed neither unjust deeds nor inappropriate ones, and as a result they appeared always open in the preaching of their doctrine to every person. For whatever they said to others and however they guided them, they exhibited the same by their own acts; and as to the hearers, who saw that their acts were in accord with their words, many became

[58] In the Syriac text this word is "prefects." However, in both versions the word makes reference to those who belonged to the ministry of the church.

their disciples without urging, and confessed Christ the King, praising God who had turned them to Him.

Many years after the death of King Abgar, one of his disobedient sons,[59] who was not submissive to the truth, arose and sent word to Aggai, when he was sitting in the Church: “Make me headbands of gold, like those which you made for my forefathers.”

Aggai spoke to him the following: “I shall not desert the ministry of Christ, which has been entrusted upon me by the disciple of Christ, and make headbands of impiety.”[60] And when he saw that Aggai had not obeyed him, he sent for him, and broke his legs, as he was sitting in the church preaching. And as he was dying, he made Palut and Barshelama swear that they would bury him in that house, for whose name he was about to die. And as he made them swear, they placed him within the middle door of the church, between the men and the women. And there was great and bitter sorrow in all the church, and all over

---

[59] According to scholars, it appears that this unjust, autocratic son did not reign until years after the death of King Abgar. There must evidently have been another, who was the immediate successor of Abgar, most likely Ma’nu, who is said to have reigned seven years, according to what is stated by Assemani, *Bibl. Orient*, Vol I, p. 421. The successor of Ma’nu was his brother, whose name was also Ma’nu, who reigned for fourteen years. Moses of Khoren, *Liv.* II. ch. xxxiv., says of him the following, “Il ouvrit les temples des idoles, embrassa le culte des païens. Il envoie dire à Attée, 'Fais moi une coiffure en toile tissée d'or, comme celles que tu faisais autrefois pour mon père.' Il reçut cette réponse d'Attée: 'Mes mains ne feront point de coiffure pour un prince indigne, qui n' adore pas le Christ Dieu vivant.' Aussitôt, le roi d'ordonner à un de ses gens d'armes de couper les pieds à Attée. Le soldat étant allé et ayant vu le saint personnage assis dans la chaire doctorale, avec son glaive lui coupa les jambes, et aussitôt le saint rendit l'esprit.”

[60] In the Syriac text this word is in the plural (“impieties”).

the city: there was indeed much anguish and inner torment, more than when Addai the Apostle died.

Since the crushing of his legs killed him swiftly and unexpectedly, he was unable to place the hand of the priesthood on Palut. Palut himself went to Antioch, and received the hand of the priesthood from Serapion, Bishop of Antioch. Serapion, Bishop of Antioch, himself received the hand of the priesthood from Zephyrinus, Bishop of the city of Rome, from the succession of the hand of the priesthood of Simon Cephas, which he received from our Master, who was there Bishop of Rome for twenty-five years, in the days of Caesar, who ruled Rome for thirteen years.

And as is the custom in the country of King Abgar, and in all kingdoms, that everything which the king commands, and everything that is said before him is written down and placed in the archives, so also Labubna, the son of Sennac, the son of Abshadar, the royal scribe, wrote these words about Addai the Apostle, from the beginning to the end. Then Hanan, the keeper of the archives, put the hand of witness, and placed it in the archives containing all royal documents, wherein are kept the commands and laws, and the contracts of those who buy and sell, being kept with great care and without any negligence.

THE END OF THE DOCTRINE
OF ADDAI THE APOSTLE.

www.ingramcontent.com/pod-product-compliance
Ingram Content Group UK Ltd.
Pitfield, Milton Keynes, MK11 3LW, UK
UKHW041834200726
13854UKWH00003BA/1135